The Origin and Nature of Tin Bounds

or; Mining Rights of the Cornish Tin Miners

Presented by Kerby Jackson

with an introduction by Kerby Jackson

Introduction

It has often been said that *"gold is where you find it"*, but even beginning prospectors understand that their chances for finding something of value in the earth or in the streams of the Golden West are dramatically increased by going back to those places where gold and other minerals were once mined by our forerunners. Despite this, much of the contemporary information on local mining history that is currently available is mostly a result of mere local folklore and persistent rumors of major strikes, the details and facts of which, have long been distorted. Long gone are the old timers and with them, the days of first hand knowledge of the mines of the area and how they operated. Also long gone are most of their notes, their assay reports, their mine maps and personal scrapbooks, along with most of the surveys and reports that were performed for them by private and government geologists. Even published books such as this one are often retired to the local landfill or backyard burn pile by the descendents of those old timers and disappear at an alarming rate. Despite the fact that we live in the so-called "Information Age" where information is supposedly only the push of a button on a keyboard away, true insight into mining properties remains illusive and hard to come by, even to those of us who seek out this sort of information as if our lives depend upon it. Without this type of information readily available to the average independent miner, there is little hope that our metal mining industry will ever recover.

This important volume and others like it, are being presented in their entirety again, in the hope that the average prospector will no longer stumble through the overgrown hills and the tailing strewn creeks without being well informed enough to have a chance to succeed at his ventures.

Kerby Jackson
Josephine County, Oregon
May 2018

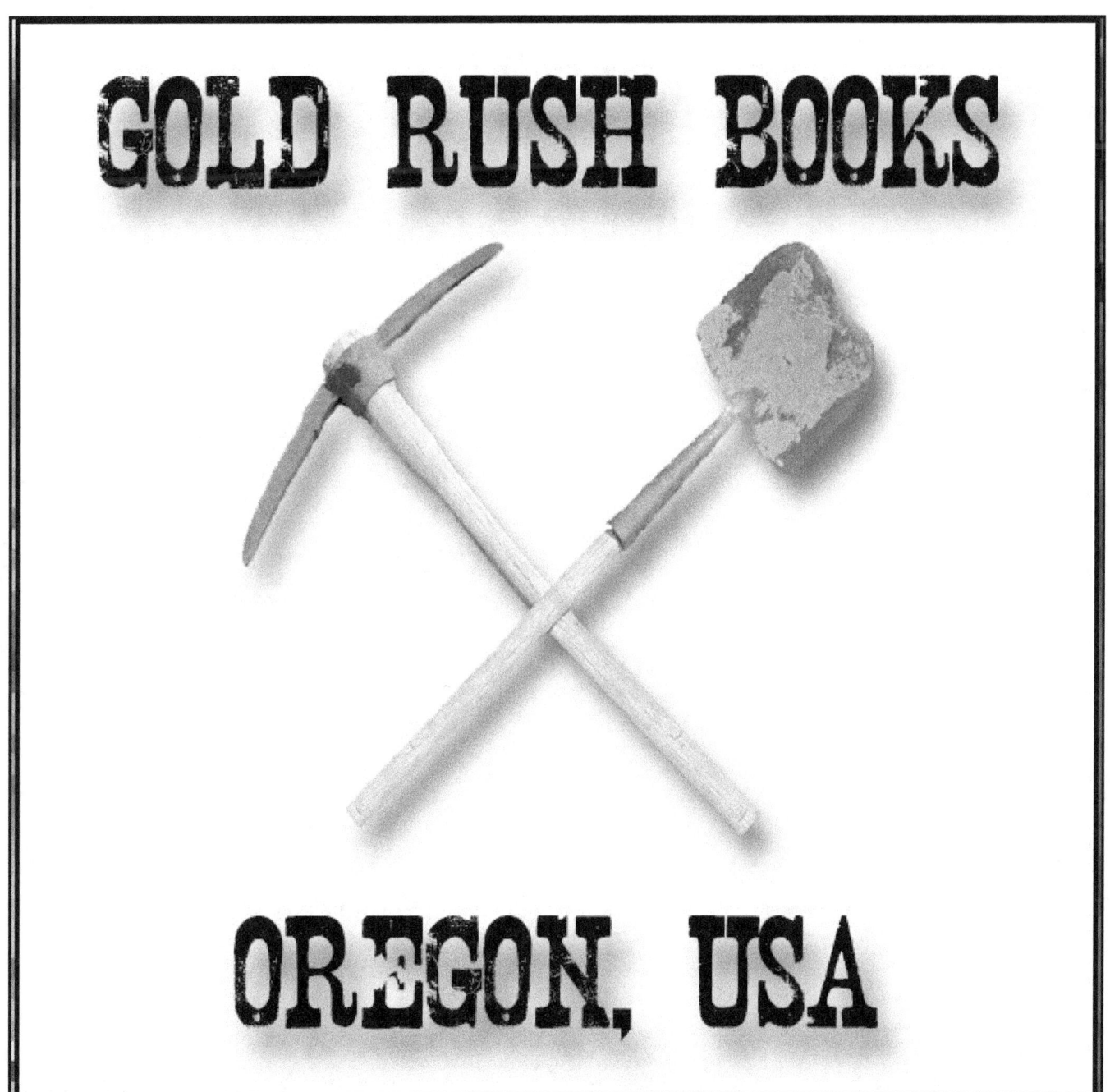

www.GoldMiningBooks.com

INQUIRY INTO THE ORIGIN AND NATURE

OF

"TIN BOUNDS."

[Extracted from No. XXVI., Vol. VI., of the "MINING REVIEW"—New Series.]

In order to understand with sufficient clearness the origin and nature of that peculiar species of property known by the name of Tin Bounds, it will be necessary to ascend in our inquiries to a remote period, and to consider the earlier history of mining under the Roman empire.

By the civil law, all veins and mineral deposits of gold or silver ore, or of precious stones, belonged, if in public ground, to the sovereign, and were part of his patrimony; if in private property, they belonged to the owner of the soil, subject to the condition, that, if worked by the owner, he was bound to render a tenth part of the produce to the prince, as a right attaching to his crown; and that, if worked by any other person, by consent of the owner, the former was liable to the payment of two-tenths—one to the prince and one to the owner of the soil.

In those countries which were annexed to the Roman empire the precious metals were the exclusive property of the sovereign prince. Thus we find that the rich mines of Spain, Thrace, and Upper Egypt, when these countries fell into the hands of the Romans, were farmed out, like most other sources of public revenue. They were chiefly mines of gold and silver, the work of which was done by slaves and state criminals.*

The reason given by ancient writers for this appropriation of the precious metals is, that all metals are applicable to the use of the public, who ought not to be prejudiced by any impediment thrown in the way of discovering and working them. They also allege that the products of mines being amongst the most precious which the earth affords, ought to be set apart for the sovereign himself,

---

* Deod. Sic. v., 38.

whose coffers being thus enriched he will be enabled to lighten the burdens of the people.*

At a later period there is reason to believe that the obligation of working mines was attached to the inhabitants of the districts in which they were situated, as is the case in Siberia, and throughout the Turkish empire at present; such was the condition of the mines in Thrace, in the reign of the Emperor Valens, when the miners abandoned their works, and joined the victorious Goths.

Trajan instituted a corporation of mining adventurers under the denomination of *Collegium Aurariorum*, for working the gold mines of Dacia; and Valentinian the First gave permission to open new mines, on consideration of his receiving a certain portion of the produce. Towards the end of the Republic there are traces of private persons being the proprietors of mines, as was also the case at a much later period.

The revenue which was drawn from this source, as well as from salt works, rivers, forests, and other branches of the *Prerogativa Regis*, was annexed to the fisc, and placed under the administration of the *Comes Sacer Largitionum*, subject to whom, in the eastern provinces, was a *Comes Metallorum*. But these were merely officers of the fiscal revenue, and appear to have had no jurisdiction over the mines; nor does it appear that any code of mining laws was ever enacted by the Romans.

How long this impost on the produce of mines continued to be levied is uncertain. It probably subsisted until the mines partook of the general ruin of the Western Empire, during the irruptions of the barbarous nations. The mines being then abandoned, and the Imperial Government at an end, no revenue could have been raised from this source during a period of considerable length. Upon the breaking up of the Roman empire, the princes and states which declared themselves independent, appropriated to themselves certain tracts of country, and subdivided them amongst their followers and dependents, subject to certain conditions and reservations. Amongst the latter was an exception of a fixed portion of the produce of mines.

When Charlemagne had established something like the form and extent of the old Roman empire, and it accorded with the policy of the papal see to sanction the delusion of its revival, a claim was advanced by the German emperor to all the royalties (regalia) which had belonged to his alleged predecessors—among which, as has been observed, was the tenth of the produce of the mines. Charlemagne exercised this right in respect only to such mines as were situated within his own domains; but Frederic Barbarossa attempted to establish it in its fullest extent. Although the tenth

---

* Gambon, vol. i., p. 50; Pearce, 9; Plowden, 315.

of the produce of mines was all that could fairly be claimed on the hypothesis of an interrupted succession, yet the mines themselves began to be considered about this time as fiscal property, and they were disposed of in various Imperial grants, and feoffments made to the princes of the empire. This assumed right was based on a false interpretation of the Roman law.

Justinian appears to have regarded the mines, according to the spirit of the more ancient Roman law, as private property—the use of which was unrestrained. There were, however, some ordinances of preceding emperors, which granted the right of opening mines in consideration of a certain impost payable to the public treasury. Although these ordinances ought to be regarded as exceptions to the general rule, applied to particular cases, yet some lawyers have deduced therefrom the extension of a right or royalty over all mines—following, in this respect, the doctors of the Bolognian school, who in their times flattered the ambitious views of the so-' vereigns of Italy as to the extent of the rights and prerogatives of the Imperial dignity.

The establishment of this doctrine led to the most important modifications of the public law of Germany during the middle ages; and one of these changes so produced, according to the opinion of Hullmann, in his " History of the Origin of Regalia in Germany," was the assumption of the Imperial right to the royalty of mines, which right had till then been exercised only as a dominical privilege, and, in particular instances, Frederic Barbarossa first established this prerogative under the new title of Regalia, or Royalties throughout Germany.

To this period of freedom in the history of mining, may be traced the mining laws of all the states of Germany. They were originally the production of free mining associations, suggested by circumstances, as they arose, recorded at first in the memories of the old, afterwards digested and committed to writing, and, finally revised and confirmed by the several princes who ruled over those states.

The sort of customary legislation which has been alluded to was not disturbed by the interference of any German prince or emperor during the period which has been mentioned, for, although Charlemagne may have caused the mines on his own domains to be worked on his own account, and the Emperor Frederic claimed the royalty of all the mines in Germany, yet the mining laws which were enacted in these primitive times were not altered or set aside by any positive or direct interference of the Emperors. The German princes forbore to meddle with them till a much later period, when some of those princes being formally invested by the Emperors with the feudal rights over the countries which they governed, and others having arbitrarily possessed themselves of those rights, they felt a direct interest in the management of mines; and the manner in which they interfered in mining concerns, as legislators, plainly shows what was the original constitution of those mines; for instance, the oldest written laws of the different German States, on the subject of mines, bear evident marks of the unwritten law of custom, and of their having been collected and compiled, as well as ratified and published, by those princes. The most ancient of these were the mining laws of Iglaw, a mining town in the confines of Moravia and Bohemia, which are still preserved in some public libraries, and which have several times appeared in print. They received the ratification of the King of Bohemia and of the Margraff of Moravia in the years 1248 and 1253, but not before they had been considerably modified and adapted to the feudal form of government which was then established.

The royalty of mines was unquestionably exercised at an early period, as a feudal or usufructuary right, but the fiscal exaction of the tenth of the produce of mines may have been of a later date, and was, no doubt, grounded on the before-mentioned hypothesis of an uninterrupted continuation of the rights and prerogatives of the Roman emperors. At present the possession of this right of royalty enables the prince who holds it, either *in capite* or by substitution, to open mines in the lands of any of his subjects; but the right extends not over all minerals, and the rule is different in different states—for instance, in Bohemia and Moravia it extends only to mines of gold and silver, but in most of the Prussian States all minerals are reserved.

It follows, from what has been stated, that the landowners are not at liberty to open mines in their own grounds, without the consent of the Sovereign. They are, however, admitted to a participation in the produce of such mines, and this in certain proportions, which vary according to the nature of that produce, and the particular law in each state. In some countries the tenth is equally divided between the prince and the landowner, and there are some minerals of which no portion is claimed by the former. The tenth is likewise modified according to the circumstances of the mine, and sometimes it is entirely relinquished until all the costs are paid, as is frequently the case in Cornwall to this day.

Having thus shortly detailed the rights of the Roman emperors to mines, and the laws of mining, which were introduced into the states of Germany, founded in a great measure on the civil code, we proceed to inquire into some particulars of the mining ordinances of Spain, which has probably derived more riches from its mineral productions than any other European nation. The course pursued by the Romans with regard to the mines of Spain is mentioned in the First Book of the Maccabees, ch. viii., v. 3.

The same plan has been since adopted by the sovereigns of

Spain, in their Transatlantic possessions, as well as in the Peninsula. Some of those mines were reserved as their exclusive property, whilst others were granted to their subjects with a reservation of the fifth, tenth, or twentieth part of the produce.

The rights of the kings of Spain to all mines were so firmly established that they were held not to pass in a grant of the land, although not excepted; and no king could grant them longer than his own life—a most wholesome restriction, and one which it is hoped Parliament will impose on the Duchy of Cornwall when application shall be made for renewal of the power of leasing, which is at present far too extensive.

The metals were expressly mentioned in the laws to be "reserved to the Sovereign, for maintaining him in honour, for defending his territories, for supporting his wars against the enemies of the faith, and relieving the people from taxes." *

The rigour of this law was moderated by John the First, but was restored by Philip the Second, who vested all mines, wherever situate, and whether in public or private ground, in the Crown, The right of search was still extended to all descriptions of persons. who, without license from the Crown, or any other party, were at liberty to try for mines in all places whatsoever.

By the second ordinance of Philip the Second, he grants permission to all persons, whether natives or foreigners, to search for mines, and declares that they should be theirs in right of possession and property, and that they may dispose of them, as of any thing of their own, subject to the payment of a portion of the produce to the Crown.

Charles the Fifth and Philip the Second made similar grants of mines in the Indies, and Spanish writers are much divided in opinion, owing to the very extensive terms of those grants, whether the mines had not thereby become the absolute property of the subject.

Without further entering into details, it is sufficient for the purpose of illustration, to state that, in South America, Spain, and the different kingdoms of Europe, a property in mines is recognised as a distinct interest from an ownership of the soil. In one respect the old law of Spain has undergone an important alteration. No part of the produce of mines is now payable to the owner of the property; the only payment required being the impost claimed by the state, and which varies according to the situation and prospects of the adventurer.†

Such is the law of Spain as respects the produce of mines. The ordinances lay down with great exactness the mode in which mines shall be worked and retained by the discoverer, and these will be

---

* Gamboa's Comm., vol. i., p. 17.　　† Gamboa, vol. i., 131.

found to correspond in a very striking and precise manner with the regulations for cutting and preserving tin bounds. The basis of a title to mines is the registry, which is nothing more than a public description of the person who has found the vein of ore and the place where it is situated, made before a justice or notary. The practice in the mining district of New Spain is to present a written document, stating the particulars above-mentioned, and the signs by which the mine may be known, setting forth the names and stakes of other proprietors continuous to it; the justice declares the mine to be registered, and gives permission to work it; after which, the applicant must sink it to a certain depth—he prays to have possession given to him, and the boundaries assigned. No mine can be lawfully worked until registry—without which it is liable to be registered by any other person.

Spanish * commentators are very diffuse on the propriety of a register, as directed by the ordinances, and Gamboa gives no less than seven substantive reasons for the regulation.

1. The recognition of the paramount rights of the crown.
2. The necessity of notice thereby given to the officers of the revenue.
3. To prevent confusion in the title to mines.
4. Because no mine ought to be opened without some strong ground for supposing it would be productive, and, consequently, to protect the interests of third persons, namely, the owners of the soil.
5. The expediency of the limits or boundaries being publicly known.
6. To ensure an early preference in measuring the limits; and
7. To prevent an interference with the rights of other mines.

The most obvious and important object attained by a registry, so far as the state is concerned, consists in the facility afforded of having an account of all the mines, and the authentic information thereby afforded concerning them, and their produce.

All the registries were recorded in the books of the mining administrator of each district, and copies transmitted to the office of the principal accountant every six months. A new registry was necessary on every change of owner, and also upon an alteration in the boundaries. No miner could take two contiguous mines, but any person might hold any number, if acquired by descent or purchase. The mode of settling the limits, viz., by fixed stakes, is very clearly laid down. The number of varas which may be included in each mine differed in different districts, and according to the particular metal discovered. The principal object in all countries appears to have been to ensure the effectual and anti-piratical working of the ground, and we shall see, by-and-bye, that this is a strong feature in the bounding system of Cornwall. It is much to be regretted that many wholesome provisions of the Stannary laws have been

---

* Gamboa, 143.

disregarded, and more especially that no correct register of tin bounds has been kept by the stewards, as was clearly the intention of the Stannators.

It is admitted by historians that Cornwall has always been celebrated for its production of tin; the jealous endeavours to monopolise the trade in that necessary article by the Phœnicians are recorded by Strabo. The Greeks next, and afterwards the Romans, sought the shores of Britain, which subsequently for a considerable period was the only country which produced this metal. The uninterrupted working of our tin mines during the Decline and Fall of the Roman Empire has been satisfactorily traced by Mr. Hawkins,* and it may be fairly presumed that certain local customs and usages prevailed at that remote period, though little is known of the regulations under which the mines were wrought until after the Norman Conquest.

The exclusive right to all mines which had been assumed by the Sovereigns of Europe, was first introduced into this island by its Norman Conquerors, but it was soon found an impolitic or useless prerogative, and was tacitly conceded to those who by the law of Nature were best entitled to it. †

The Norman earls derived immense revenues from these mines, but they were afterwards much neglected, and in the reign of John the produce was very trifling; under the management of the Jews who farmed the tin mines in the succeeding reign, Earl Richard was enabled to amass immense riches, which he transmitted in waggons to Germany, and which gained for him the empty title of King of the Romans. When the Jews were banished, the tin mines became again neglected, and Earl Edmund, the son of Richard, granted the mines a charter, which is not now extant, but its principal provisions are supposed to have been embodied in subsequent grants and the Acts of Convocation.

We proceed to extract from the documentary evidence now in existence such parts as may throw a light on the subject immediately under review.

The earliest charter in existence relating to the Stannaries is the 3d John, A.D. 1202, which is preserved in the Tower of London among the Records of the Court of Chancery.‡ In the charter power is given to " all our tinners in Cornwall and Devon, that they may at all times freely and quietly, without the disturbance of any man, dig tin, and turves to melt their tin, any where in the moors, and in the fees of bishops, abbots, earls, *as they have used and been accustomed* "—recognising in the latter sentence an existing custom, which must necessarily have originated before the

---

* " Transactions of the Geological Society of Cornwall," vol. iv.
† Hawkins, " Transactions of the Geological Society of Cornwall," vol. iv., 27.
‡ 3 Mann. and Ryl., 493.

commencement of legal memory. The charter goes on to exempt the tinners from the jurisdiction of any officer except the Custos or Lord Warden and his bailiffs, and confers a power of diverting waters to enable them to carry on their mining operations. It also confers other and important privileges.

The 33d Edward I., described by Pearce " as the first charter * for creating the tinners of Cornwall into a corporation," confirms to tinners all their ancient and exclusive rights, and, amongst other things, declares " we have granted also to the said tinners that they may dig tin, and turves to melt tin, any where in the lands, moors, and wastes, of us and of others whomsoever 'in the county aforesaid, and divert waters and water-courses for the works of the Stannaries aforesaid, where and when it shall be necessary, and buy wood to melt the tin *as they have been accustomed*, without hindrance of us or of our heirs, bishops, abbots, priors, earls, barons, and others whomsoever." These charters establish the fact of an existence by custom, at that very remote period, of a right to search for tin in the demesnes of the Earls of Cornwall as well as in the lands of individuals.

In the several subsequent charters, the rights and privileges conceded by the 3d John and the 33d Edward I., are confirmed, and it is unnecessary to to refer more particularly to them ; we proceed at once to the grant of pardon, in the 23d Henry VII., which is a very important document. Pearce gives the following history of this charter :- Prince Arthur, eldest son to King Henry VII., made certain constitutions relating to the Stannaries, which the tinners refusing to observe, and taking greater liberty than was justifiable by their charters, King Henry VII. (who seldom let slip any opportunity of filling his coffers) made that a pretence, after Prince Arthur's death, to secure the Stannaries into his own hands, but finding that it did not turn to such account as he expected, was prevailed upon to accept of 1000*l.* for all the pretended forfeitures, granting them his charter of pardon. †

In the Act of Convocation, 30th Elizabeth, a similar account of the origin of this charter is given :—" We find, also, that Prince Arthur, eldest son unto King Henry VII., ordained not only divers penal ordinances against tinners before-named, but also against divers persons intermeddling with black and white tin, by reason of which penal ordinances they incurred divers forfeitures ; for redemption whereof, by petition and payment of 1000*l.* to the king, they obtained the king's pardon."—Sect. 4.‡

This charter purports to " pardon, remise, and release, Robert

---

* The tinners of Cornwall were by this grant made a separate body from those of Devon—they had hitherto been united.

† Preface xi.   ‡ M.S. in the Duchy office.

Willoughby, Lord de Brooke, John Mohun, Esq., John Godolphin, Esq., James Erisey, gent., and others, amounting, in the whole, to 1500 persons, with the several additions of knights, esquires, and gentlemen," otherwise called "tinners, bounders, or possessors of works of tin; and to the bounder, or possessor of any tin-work, in the county of Cornwall, who have not, or hath not, introduced the names of new possessors, or a new possessor, of any tin-work newly bounded, with the names of the works in the next Court of Stannary after the bounding aforesaid, showing the names or name of the possessors or possessor of the same works or work of tin, with the metes and bounds of the said works or work, as well in length as in breadth;" and for other offences against the Stannary laws, particularly enumerated, " all transgressions, contempts, impeachments, forfeitures, concealments, fines, pains, imprisonments, amerciaments, debts and losses adjudged, or to be adjudged, abuses, retentions, and offences against the form of any statutes, ordinances, provisions, restrictions, or proclamations by us, or by our progenitors, before this time made."—"Rowe v. Brenton," 3 Manning and Ryland, p. 213.

Two important facts are clearly established by this charter—the existence of tin bounds *eo. nomine*, and a possession by a peer of the realm and others, the most distinguished names in the aristocracy of the county, thus satisfactorily proving that tin bounds were not originally (as it has been contended) the exclusive property of the *stannator operans*, or working tinner.

It has been argued that the tinners had forfeited their liberties and privileges in this reign, and that we must not ascend higher in our inquiries for information as to their extent and origin, but date the present system from this charter. This argument may be easily disposed of. We deny the legality of the assumed original forfeiture; but, admitting its validity, does not the charter confer, on its face, an unqualified and entire restitution?

The charter of Henry VII. first mentions the mode of acquiring a property in tin bounds, but we must seek a fuller explanation in the different acts of the Stannary Parliaments, or Convocation of Tinners.

All tinners having by custom, confirmed by charters, a right to search for tin throughout the Stannaries, it seems to follow as a necessary consequence that certain regulations were necessary to limit the extent of each man's work, and to ascertain the rights of those who had first discovered the minerals, or were disposed to bestow their labour in the search. It is preposterous to suppose that, even in its earliest operations, mining was without a system which afforded to the labourer a probability that the benefit of his discoveries to-day would not become the property of a stranger to-morrow.

To secure such benefit, under certain regulations, and to prevent the inextricable confusion which would arise from a different course of proceeding, was undoubtedly the object and basis of the bounding system of Cornwall. Nor is this practice confined to the Stannaries. In every mining district a custom exists similar in many essential particulars to that of our tin bounds in other countries; indeed, the right is more extensive, and it may be considered oppressive. The power to enter and search for minerals, which by custom and the charter was not confined to any particular description of ground, is by the Stannary laws limited to waste and uncultivated lands, or such as have been originally wastrell.

On the Continent, in South America, no exception is known. In Derbyshire, and elsewhere in England, the landowner possesses no power to control workings which do not absolutely interfere with his dwelling-house, garden, or orchard. I extract an article from the laws enacted at the Great Barrmote Court, held for the wapentake of Wirksworth, in the year 1665 :—" We say, by the custom of the mine within the wapentake of Wirksworth, 'tis lawful for all liege people of this nation to dig, delve, subvert, mine, and turn up all manner of grounds, lands, meadows, closes, pastures, moores, or marshes, for lead ore, within the said wapentake, of whose inheritance soever it is—dwelling-house, highways, orchards, or gardens excepted."—" Appendix to the Mineral Laws and Customs of Derbyshire," page 89.

I will now proceed to give a brief description of a tin bound, and of the mode of setting out, or, as the tinners term it, " cutting bounds," and the regulations to be observed in preserving and keeping the same, as prescribed by the Stannary laws.

Having fixed on a waste plot of ground of reasonable dimensions, in which there is a prospect of finding tin, and which is preferred when it is near a stream of water, the bounder cuts out four corners in right angles to each other, and at each corner cuts up six turfs, and places them as hillocks ; these mark the limits or boundaries of the enclosure within which he is to work, and by the Stannary laws these hillocks are to be renewed every year, on the anniversary of the day on which they were first cut, which is called " renewing the bounds." A declaration, styled a *Proclamation of Bounds*, is then drawn up, describing the situation of the bounds, the day on which they were cut, and if, as is most commonly the case, the proceeding be conducted by an agent, the latter states the names and descriptions of his employers, and that the spot then marked out was void of lawful bounds.

The following is a literal copy of a proclamation of bounds :—

" Cur. 18th Maii, 1725.

" *Stannary de Penwith and Kirrier.*

" This court gives notice of one pair of tyn bounds, void of all lawfull bounds, cutt the eleventh day of May by Bennett Uren, to the use of Jonathan Hill, Esq., Otho Glynn, gent., William, the son of William Thomas, and Elizabeth, the daughter of Thomas Watts, in the parishe of Wendron, in the said Stannary, called by name of Come sooner next, the N.E. corner whereof joyneth with the highway leading from Porthkellis to Hallwen; the N.W. corner lyes nigh a worke called Samuel Dunstone's worke; the S.E. corner lyes nigh Hallwen Moor; and the S.W. corner adjoins with Downandevers, as by the bounds and limitts thereof do appear.

1725.—18th Maii, prima procland.
    8th Junii, secunda procland.
    29th Junii, tertia procland, et judicand.

The following is a translation of the Writ of Possession founded on the foregoing proclamation; the original is in Latin, as were all proceedings in the Steward's Court until the year 1730, when by the 4th Geo. II., cap. 26, all law proceedings were ordered to be "done into English." [And here it may be observed, that a strong argument in proof of the antiquity of the equitable jurisdiction exercised by the Vice Warden is derived from the fact that whilst proceedings in the Stewards' Courts were in Latin, those in the Court of the Vice-Warden were in English—thus assimilated to the practice which distinguished the equitable and common law courts at Westminster.

In early times "Law and Latin," "English and Chancery," were synonomous terms, so much so, that the *law* side of the Court of Chancery was called the *Latin* side; the *equity* side of the Court of Chancery was termed the *English* side.]

    " Writ of Possession of Come sooner next Bounds.

    " *Stannary of Penwith and Kirrier.*

    " Hugh Lord Falmouth, Lord Keeper and Warden of the Stannaries, Chief Steward of the Duchy of Cornwall, and so forth;

" To the bailiff of the Stannary of Penwith and Kirrier, and also to Stephen Trenoweth, John Ellis, Edward Chilcott, and every of them, greeting, Whereas, Benedict Uren came to the court, held for the said Stannary of Penwith and Kirrier, on the 18th day of May, A.D. 1725, and gave notice to the said court that he had, on the 11th day of May then instant, bounded one piece of ground, called "Come sooner next," in the parish of Wendron, within the said Stannary, void of all lawful bounds, to the use of Jonathan Hill, Esq., Otho Glynn, gent., William, the son of William Thomas, and Elizabeth, the daughter of Thomas Watts. The N.E. corner of the said bounds joins the highway leading from Porkellis to Hallwen; the N.W. corner lies near a tin-work called "Samuel Dunstone's work;" the S.E. corner lies near Hallwen Moor; and the S.W. corner adjoins Downandevers. And the said Benedict Uren desired proclamation of the said bounds to be made according to the custom of the Stannaries; and because no one came to the first, second, or third courts, to deny proclamation thereof to be made, and to claim an interest in the said bounds, called "Come sooner next," therefore, at the court held for the said Stannary of Penwith and Kirrier, on the 29th day of June, 1725, it was adjudged, by the said court, that the said Jonathan Hill, Otho Glynn, William Thomas, and Elizabeth Watts, should recover possession of the said bounds; therefore, on behalf of George Prince of Wales and Duke of Cornwall, I command you and every of you, that, without delay, you or one of you deliver possession of the said bounds to the said Jonathan Hill, Otho Glynn, William Thomas, and Elizabeth Watts, and whatsoever you or either of you shall do in the premises, that you or one of you certify to me, or my deputy, at the next court, to be held for the said Stannary of Penwith and Kirrier.

" Given under the seal of the office of the Duchy of Cornwall, the 20th day of July, in the 11th year of the reign of our Sovereign Lord George by the grace of God of Great Britain, France, and Ireland, King, Defender of the Faith, and so forth, and in the year of our Lord 1725."

These bounds are now in the possession of the Rev. R. G. Grylls, the representative of Otho Glynn, Esq.

By the last Act of Convocation, viz., the 26th Geo. II., 1752, the bounder must give three months' notice to the lord of the soil, of his intention to cut such bounds, in order that the latter may, if he think fit, cut and work such bounds for his own benefit —in consequence of which bounds have been very rarely cut since that enactment. At the expiration of such notice, the bounder proceeds as before-mentioned; and at the next law court, held by the steward within the particular Stannary in which the bounds are situate, a minute description of the land and limits is entered by the steward, who causes proclamation to be made, in order that if any objection can be raised to the bounder's claim, it may be decided by a jury of tinners. Any person is at liberty to urge an objection to the bounder's claim, and justice may be reasonably expected to result from an inquiry conducted on the constitutional principle of trial by jury. Notice is then stuck up in the court, and proclamation is repeated at three successive sittings, each held at an interval of three weeks; at the last of which, if no person, either lord or stranger, shall appear and contest the claim, the bounder obtains judgment, and a Writ of Possession issues under the seal of the court, directed to the bailiff of the Stannary, who goes publicly on the spot and delivers possession accordingly. The title of the bounder is then complete.

The reader will not fail to remark the strong coincidence between the process detailed above, and the mode of acquiring property in the earlier history of the world; the means of which the right of the bounder is perfected, corresponds in a striking manner with the rules laid down for the transfer of lands by the ancients. Among the Jews a symbolical delivery of possession was required. " With our Saxon ancestors the delivery of a *turf* was a necessary solemnity to establish the conveyance of lands." (2 Bl. 313.) And at this day the transfer of some copyholds is effected by this mode. The invention of the assurance by lease and release has abolished, in practice, the ancient livery of seisin; but its necessity is still a principle of law, though effected by a more refined and convenient process.

The Stannary laws abound with salutary regulations, adopted

for the purpose of preventing a fraudulent acquisition of bounds, and an interference with the rights of others; nor is this all : they prescribe a *bonâ fide* working or renewal of property thus acquired; and in default thereof, liberty is given to others to do so after proper notice. We proceed with the documentary evidence.

The Charter of Pardon has been already mentioned. We next come to the Stannary Convocation, or Parliament of Tinners, held from time to time under writs of privy seal. After defining the two descriptions of persons who were entitled to the benefit of the Stannary laws as " privileged tinners" and " tinners at large," the stannators declare their custom of bounding as follows :— " We find, that every tinner that shall new-cut any old works, ought, at the Stannary Court next following, to enter his proclamation for the same, and therein nominate all his owners, and the day of his new cut, and the old name of the same work, with bounds and limits of his new pitch, or else the new pitch to be void. We find, that tenants by courtesy, tenants in dower, or for years in wastrell, ought to be, according to ancient customs, enabled to work; and if the tinner working in the same pay tin-toll to the lord, that then the same to be adjudged a lawful tin-work, and assured, and the tinner for ever to enjoy the same, according to the custom; and that tenants in tail ought not to expel any tinner having any tin-work lately assured by working peaceably, and toll tin paid. We find that, if any person being specially appointed to renew bounds, do by coven between him and the new bounder, misuse the confident trust reposed in him, and do suffer the old bounders to become void, that then the same ought to make a remitter to all the old bounders and owners."

By the 22d James I., the following regulations are re-enacted :— " We find, according to our ancient customs, that every tinner that shall new-cut any old bounds, shall, at the next court within the Stannary where the work is, enter his proclamation for the same, and therein nominate all his owners, and the day of his pitch, and the names, both old and new, of the said work, with the bounds and limits of the said pitch, otherwise the said pitch to be deemed void."

In the 12th Charles I. another Convocation was held, and the following clauses relate to bounding :—" We present and affirm that, by common prescribed Stannary right, any tinner may bound any wastrel lands within the county of Cornwall that is unbounded, or void of lawful bounds; and also any several and enclosed land that hath been anciently bounded and assured for wastrel, by delivering of toll-tin to the lord of the soil, before that the hedges were made upon it; and also such and so much of the Prince's assessionable manors as hath been anciently bounded with turfs, according to the ancient custom and usage within the said several duchy manors, and not otherwise; the tinner paying out of such land so bounded the usual toll only as is generally paid within the Stannaries—that is, the fifteenth dish or part, saving in such places where a special custom hath limited another rate of toll. We present and affirm our general custom of gaining and keeping right in bounds to be by new pitch, and renew in such manner as it now is, and anciently hath been, in use, in the several Stannaries; which said general custom we limit, ordain, and agree, that it shall be thus understood, viz., that an owner working his tin-work by himself, his wages-man or farmer paying toll once a year and a day, or otherwise continuing his working without fraud, in driving an adit unto or sinking a shaft upon the said work, and withal preserving the four corner bounds, so as they be seen or sufficiently proved, if they or any of them shall be newly, or casually, or maliciously, defaced, so long the said owner shall not lose his bounds for default of renewing. We agree, constitute, and ordain, that whosoever shall pitch any bounds, shall enter his proclamation for the same in the Stannary Court where the ground lieth, at the first court that shall be holden after the said pitch; in which proclamation he shall set down the day of the pitch, the names of his fellow-owners, the name of the said work, and the old name also, together with the place where the bounds lie, or otherwise the pitch to be void."

And by sec. 31st it is provided, that in case any bounds shall be unwrought for the space of seven years, and any tinner shall be desirous to work the same, he shall be at liberty so to do on giving notice to the owners, and making certain entries in the Stewards' Court.

The next Convocation was held in the 4th James II., 1687, and the regulations for cutting and renewing bounds are very fully stated, and a remedy given by action of trespass to any person who should, in any of the three courts, when proclamation was made, advance a claim to the bounds intended to be cut.

By the fourth section, bounds are declared to be by *custom* a chattle real, which should be perpetually enjoyed from executor to executor, or administrator, and be executory assets, subject to the payment of debts and legacies.

The last Convocation was held at Truro, in the 26th Geo. II., 1752. The third section of the 11th Charles I. is re-enacted *totidem verbis*, and several salutary provisions are made to prevent fraud between bounders, and to regulate the conduct of their agents. The third section is very important. It recites that tin bounds or tin works in bounds had lain unwrought for many years, to the great prejudice of the Stannaries. It then enacts, that if any bounds should remain unwrought for the space of twelve months, and any person should be desirous to work for tin within such bounds, he should signify his intention to the owner or his agent, and make the proper entries in the Stewards' Court. If such owner neglected to work the bounds within two months, the person giving notice might enter and work, as if he had a sett, on giving security, by bond, with two sureties, to work the ground effectually.

Notice of an intention to cut bounds, which was required to be given to the lord of the soil by the Act of James II., is reduced from one year to three months, at the end of which the person desirous of working might enter and cut bounds, and enjoy the same according to the laws and customs of the Stannaries.

A new and important provision is introduced in this Act of Convocation, having for its object to ensure a *bonâ fide* working of bounds to be thereafter cut. It is enacted, that if the owner of any bounds *thereafter to be cut* should not, within three years after proclamation passed, deliver toll tin to the lord of the soil in which the bounds were situate, or at least proceed and continue effectually to work the same, such bounds should be void. The bounder is also required to show the corners, and day of renewal, to any lord of the soil, or to his toller or agent.

Tin bounds have been recognised by the superior courts, both at *nisi prius*, and in Bane and in Rowe, and Brenton, great reliance was attached to the perception of toll tin in confirmation of the exclusive right of the duchy to copper and other minerals, " subject to the usages and customs of the Stannary laws."

Sir Charles Wetherell, in his opening speech, after describing the manner of acquiring tin bounds, said "This right or custom of bounding is equally prevalent against the Duke of Cornwall as it would be against a private individual, owner in fee."

Since " Rex *v*. St. Agnes " (3, T. R., 480), the toll and farm have been separately rated in the parish of St. Agnes, as has been the case elsewhere for a very considerable period. This is in the Duchy manor of Tywarnhayle. The Stannary roll was also produced by the Crown, in Rowe and Brenton, to prove the laws of bounding, in order to show that they identified the Duke of Cornwall as lord of the soil.

There is no mention, in the earlier charters, of any specific toll being paid to the earls, though it is clear they derived their revenues principally from a tribute paid by the miner; and we are told that the mines were farmed by the Jews, in the reign of John.

There is a return made by William, of Wrotham, in the 9th Richard I. (Rowe and Brenton, 12), which recites that there was then, by ancient custom, 30d. in Devonshire and 5s. in Cornwall payable to the King, for every 1000d weight of tin " weighed by the greater weight," *ad firman de Stannaries*, and for a toll for the carriage, &c.; but this payment seems exclusively applicable to the duty on the coinage of tin. The toll,* or proportion of ore paid to the landowner out of bounded property, is one-fifteenth, "unless where a special custom hath limited another manner of toll" (see Stannary Laws), the farm one-twelfth—but it now invariably happens that, from the great depth, and consequent expense of working mines, and other causes, these payments are reduced, in order to enable the adventurer to carry on his speculation with some chance of profit, or indemnity against the actual disbursements.

The impolicy of exacting exorbitant dues is as apparent as the practice of reserving extravagant rents—the result must inevitably prove injurious to the real interests of the granter. Hence, in our principal tin mines, the bounder grants on liberal terms, and the owner of the soil receives the same *relative proportion* of the dish as he is entitled to under the Stannary law, and in some cases he gets as much as the bounder. In the parish of St. Agnes the toll is five-twelfths, and the farm seven-twelfths, which nearly bear the same proportion to each other as do a twelfth and a fifteenth. In the parish of Wendron, the bounder and landlord divide equally, and such was proved to have been the custom in Rowe and Brenton, throughout the assessional manor of Tewington. In Rowe and Brenton, a Duchy agent was called by the Crown, who produced a tin bill, in which the division between the Duchy and the bounder was marked. We extract a passage:—" He also stated that the custom was, to divide the dues between the owner of the soil and the bounder—that there was a known distinction in Cornwall between ffee land and Duchy land, or ancient Duchy; that ancient Duchy consisted of the conventionary tenements and wastes in the seventeen manors already named—and that in ffee land the owner of the fee and the bounder; in Duchy land the lessee of the Duke and the bounder divided the dues."*

This reduction in the original dish has existed for a considerable period, and though it originated long since the commencement of legal memory, it seems to be considered an established custom, and few have attempted to dispute its legality.

It is clear that no respectable adventurer can work a tin mine in the present day, if he pay both bounder and landowner the dish to which each is legally entitled; and if the parties persevere, a natural result will be, that the whole mining population will be thrown out of employ, and the market supplied from Banca, which even now threatens to overwhelm the Cornish miner.

The bounder has the exclusive right of granting setts or licenses to work, and as a consequence the terms are settled between him-

---

* " Farm " tin is the portion payable to the bounder—" toll," to the lord of the soil out of bounded land. Lords' " dues " is a term used where no bounds exist.

self and the adventurer. It has not been any where determined what remedy the lord of the soil has against the latter—it would seem that the bounder only is answerable for the toll; there is no legal privity between the adventurer and the landlord.

The bounder clearly possesses the power to control a claim advanced by the lord of the soil to his original toll, when the prospects of the mine render it impossible that the adventurer can pay both toll and farm, as settled in early times, and when mining operations were conducted on simple and inexpensive principles.

The ordinary dish at the present day is one-fifteenth, and few tin mines can afford to pay more; if, therefore, the lord, or the Duchy lessee, claim his full toll, the bounder will get nothing, and it follows that he will, or ought to, refuse his consent, until an equitable division shall have been settled between them. The bounder being answerable for the toll, will not, it is manifest, voluntarily incur a liability without an equivalent, and his course is, therefore, to reject all overtures to work his bounds until the toll shall have been abated. The bounds must remain unwrought until the lord shall either come to his senses, or apply to the Stannary Court for license to work, which he will not be allowed to do without first entering into a bond, with two sureties, to pay the bounder his farm and to work the sett effectually.—*See* 26th Geo. II., sec. 3.

The Stannary laws are quite sufficient for the protection of the bounder, and if he will only take the trouble to look into a code, compiled by the great and good of former times, and its excellence been confirmed by the experience of ages, he need not apprehend a loss of his property, if he will apply for relief to the proper local tribunal.

The expressions in the Charter of John, *sicut hactenus fuerit usitatum*, recognises an existing custom, which no doubt corresponded with the law of other mining districts, by which the earl or lord of the soil was entitled to a portion of the produce.

It seems probable that the Norman princes claimed, and received, the part reserved by the civil law, which was occasionally varied, according to the circumstances and prospects of the particular mine. The writer has taken some pains to ascertain the origin of the fifteenth, payable under the Stannary laws, but he has been unable to find any authority beyond what may be deduced from contemporary history. Hume says—" Subsidies and *fifteenths* are frequently mentioned, but neither the amount of these taxes, nor the method of levying them, have been well explained." It appears that fifteenths formerly corresponded to the

---

* 3 Mann. and Ryl., 216.

name, and were the proportionable part of the moveables.—Vol. vi,
p. 175.

We learn from Coke, that a valuation of the kingdom was made
in the reign of Edward III., and from that time each town or district paid a certain quotum. This valuation took place in 1335,
three years before the creation of the Duchy of Cornwall, and it
seems probable that the Crown then fixed with the tinners the
payment of a specific dish or toll, which corresponded with the
general and established subsidy imposed on all his Majesty's liege
subjects.

It is foreign to our present purpose, to enter into a disquisition
on a subject necessarily involved in much obscurity, there seems
sufficient plausibility in the supposition to justify its mention here.
The expediency of a legislative enactment has been suggested, by
which tin bounds shall cease at the expiration of sixty years from
the passing of the statute, *i.e.*, the bounders property; after that
period should be merged in the paramount right of the owner of
the soil. It is scarcely conceivable on what principle this plan
could be effected. The measure would be one of unjustifiable
spoliation.

The rights of humanity found an excuse for the abolition of a
system which had been confirmed by numerous statutes—the slave
trade. The Reform Bill owed its existence to a popular outcry
against an unconstitutional interference of one branch of the Legislature with the other, and we have seen vested interests wholly
disregarded, when the public good became an argument for their
extinction—but here is no such pretence, or, if it be urged, the
reasoning will not bear the test of examination.

It has been shown elsewhere, that the object of all legislators
in mining countries has been to ensure a *bond fide* working, and
this is a principal object of the Stannary laws, which provide means
for compelling the bounder to work, or allow others to do so. No
evidence can be adduced to establish the charge, that a property
in tin bounds is injurious to the interests of the county. A few
landlords may sigh for a monopoly of the underground wealth,
and grudge the appropriation of any part to a stranger, but this
species of reasoning may be turned against themselves. Persons
may, with equal justice, question the unequal distribution of
wealth, and advocate the expediency of an Agrarian law.

If property, which originated in the earliest ages, and has re-
peatedly formed the subject of family settlements, is to be rudely
destroyed on such pretences as have been urged for the abolition
of tin bounds, no human possession would be safe.

Perhaps we shall be told that compensation will not be denied.
Compensation! Is it conceivable, that any one will attempt, or
pretend to lay down, a principle on which the mineral value of an

untried district may be fairly estimated ? A moment's consideration of the peculiar species of property sought to be destroyed, will at once satisfy us that compensation is wholly out of the question, and that any attempt to lay down a scale of remuneration must be wholly futile. Let it be remembered that the principal tin mines of this country are under bounds. Wheal Vor, for instance, has produced 500,000*l.* and upwards, and is still in full operation. Not many years since, one of the bounders offered to sell his interest in that and other mines for 100*l.*; he has since received a very large sum from Wheal Vor alone.

The gentleman alluded to might be disposed, of his own free will, to get rid of an unproductive property, and could only reproach himself if it turned out better than he had anticipated, but if the omnipotence of Parliament shall be invoked, for the purpose of destroying important and long existing interests, the owners would have serious and well-grounded cause for complaint, if they were deprived, *per vim*, of their hereditary possessions. The distinction between the existence of a supreme power in a state, and the *arbitrary* exercise of that power, ought never to be lost sight of.

"There cannot," says Junius, " be a doctrine more fatal to the liberty and property we are contending for, than that which confounds the idea of a *supreme* and an *arbitrary* Legislature. I need not point out to you the fatal purposes to which it has been, and may be, applied."

I will, in conclusion, say a few words on the charge brought against the bounder, that through his means many tin mines in this county are now idle and unwrought.

It is hardly conceivable, that a person would refuse to work, by himself or agents, or grant permission to others, land from which he can derive no benefit, except through its mineral production. A bounder has no local sympathies to gratify—no hereditary attachment to the surface; his only interest—real or imaginary—arises from *bonâ fide* workings, and there is not an instance within my knowledge, or that of persons intimately acquainted with mining operations, of whom I have made inquiries, where liberty to work has been refused by an owner of tin bounds.

Many circumstances may induce others to withhold an assent to allow mines in their property, or to extort exorbitant dues from the adventurer; self-interest—the most powerful engine in directing the conduct of man—urges the bounder to afford every facility towards making his property productive; at the same time, his cupidity is wisely checked by the wholesome provisions of the Stannary laws, which limit the dish or farm, payable out of bounds, to a fixed amount, sanctioned by custom and immemorial usage.

It has been observed, that if any fraudulent practice should be resorted to, for the purpose of obtaining or maintaining an interest in bounds, the Stannary laws afford an ample remedy, as may be seen by a reference to these laws, and of which persons may avail themselves if they think proper.

With respect to men of rank and influence in the county becoming proprietors of bounds, the Stannary laws declare that bounds are in the nature of chattels real, and may be assigned by deed, or given by will, to any person (subject still to the regulations provided by the Stannary laws), and this is every day's practice in Cornwall, so that tin bounds at present are become of considerable consequence and value to many families, particularly where mines are under bounds, and produce large quantities of tin, as in the case of Wheal Vor, the St. Ives Consolidated Mines, and others; such mines would never be worked by the manual labour of working tinners; and had it not been for the machinery introduced by the wealth and influence of persons of large property, such mines must remain idle, to the prejudice of the labouring tinner, and the diminution of the revenues of the Duchy.

It may also be observed, that most of the tin streams in Cornwall are under bounds, which afford employment and subsistence to some hundreds of the labouring tinners, and from whence the best tin in the Stannaries, called "grain tin," or "perillian tin," is collected. If the bounds on these were abolished, the landowners would, in many instances, feel it more advantageous to turn the lands into cultivation, by which the tinners would be thrown out of employ; which, however beneficial to their individual interests, would directly violate the great principle to be steadily kept in view in a mining country—viz., the encouragement to *bond fide* workings

London: Printed by R. Middleton, 12, Gough square, Fleet-street.